Uno, Dos, Tres

Let's Learn Spanish
Children's Learn Spanish Books

BABY PROFESSOR

EDUCATION KIDS

Let's learn the Spanish alphabet.

a

ah

✏ Trace the word.

ah   ah   ah

✏ Rewrite the word.

b

bay

✏ Trace the word.

bay   bay   bay

✏ Rewrite the word.

<table>
<tr><td>ENGLISH</td><td>SPANISH</td></tr>
</table>

ENGLISH	SPANISH
c	say

 Trace the word.

say   say   say

 Rewrite the word.

ENGLISH	SPANISH
ch	chay

 Trace the word.

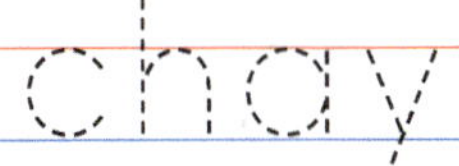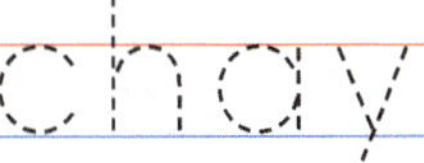

 Rewrite the word.

ENGLISH
SPANISH
d
day
Trace the word.
day   day   day
Rewrite the word.
ENGLISH
SPANISH
e
ay
Trace the word.
ay   ay   ay
Rewrite the word.

<table>
<tr><td>ENGLISH</td><td>SPANISH</td></tr>
<tr><td>f</td><td>ay-fay</td></tr>
</table>

 Trace the word.

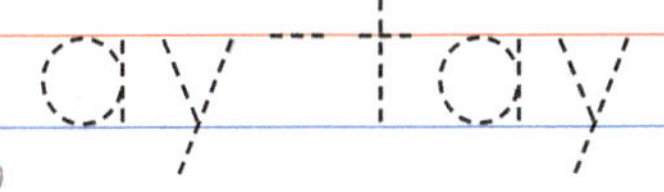 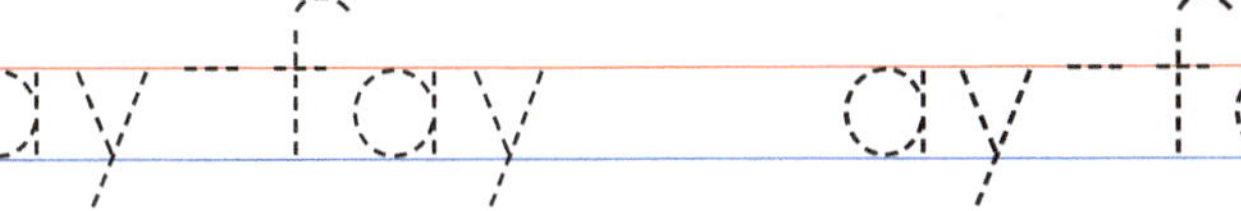

 Rewrite the word.

<table>
<tr><td>ENGLISH</td><td>SPANISH</td></tr>
<tr><td>g</td><td>hey</td></tr>
</table>

Trace the word.

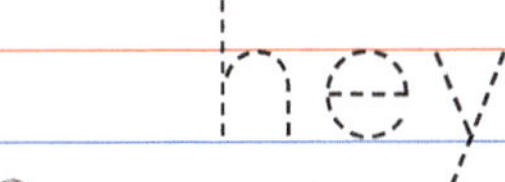  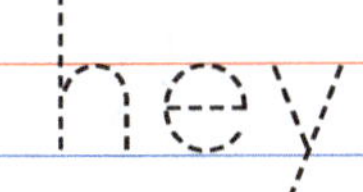

 Rewrite the word.

<table>
<tr><td>ENGLISH</td><td>SPANISH</td></tr>
<tr><td>h</td><td>ah-chay</td></tr>
</table>

 Trace the word.

ah-chay ah-chay ah-chay

 Rewrite the word.

<table>
<tr><td>ENGLISH</td><td>SPANISH</td></tr>
<tr><td>i</td><td>ee</td></tr>
</table>

 Trace the word.

ee 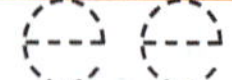 ee 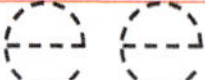 ee 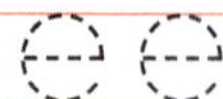

 Rewrite the word.

<table>
<tr><td>ENGLISH</td><td>SPANISH</td></tr>
</table>

ENGLISH | **SPANISH**

j | hoh-tah

 Trace the word.

hoh-tah   hoh-tah   hoh-tah

 Rewrite the word.

ENGLISH | **SPANISH**

k | kah

 Trace the word.

kah   kah   kah

 Rewrite the word.

ENGLISH
SPANISH
I
ay-lay
Trace the word.
ay-lay   ay-lay   ay-lay
Rewrite the word.

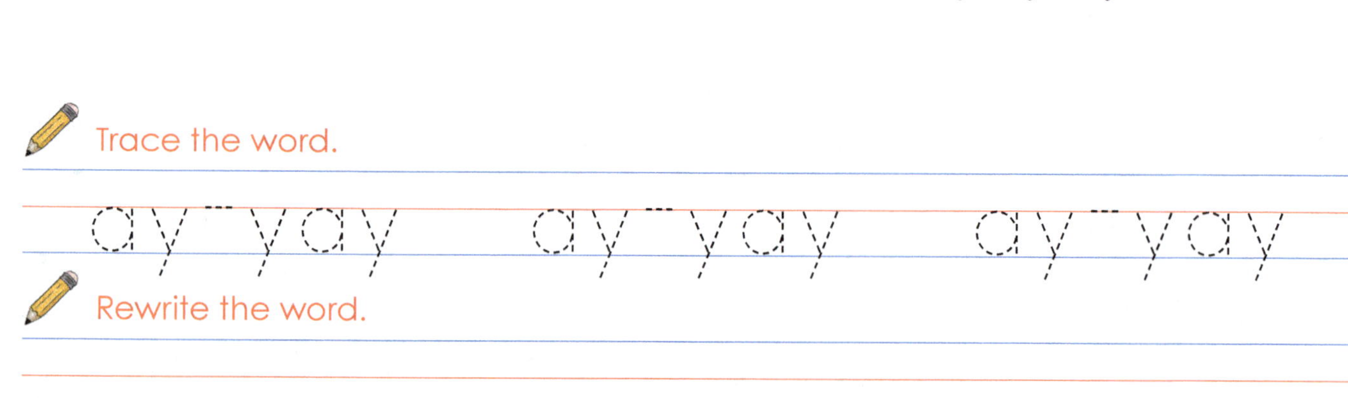

ENGLISH
SPANISH
II
ay-yay
Trace the word.
ay-yay   ay-yay   ay-yay
Rewrite the word.

<table>
<tr><td>ENGLISH</td><td>SPANISH</td></tr>
<tr><td>m</td><td>ay-may</td></tr>
</table>

 Trace the word.

ay-may   ay-may   ay-may

 Rewrite the word.

<table>
<tr><td>ENGLISH</td><td>SPANISH</td></tr>
<tr><td>n</td><td>ay-nay</td></tr>
</table>

 Trace the word.

ay-nay   ay-nay   ay-nay

Rewrite the word.

<table>
<tr><td>ENGLISH</td><td>SPANISH</td></tr>
<tr><td>ñ</td><td>ayn⁻yay</td></tr>
</table>

✏️ Trace the word.

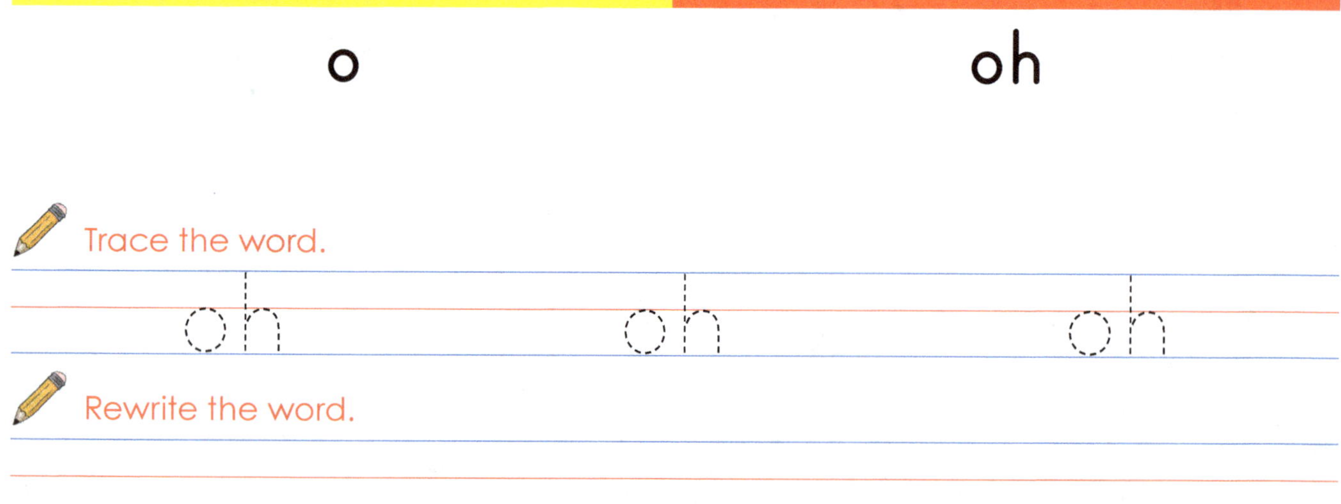

✏️ Rewrite the word.

<table>
<tr><td>ENGLISH</td><td>SPANISH</td></tr>
<tr><td>o</td><td>oh</td></tr>
</table>

✏️ Trace the word.

oh   oh   oh

✏️ Rewrite the word.

<table>
<tr><td></td><td></td></tr>
</table>

Trace the word.

Rewrite the word.

<table>
<tr><td></td><td></td></tr>
</table>

Trace the word.

Rewrite the word.

ENGLISH	SPANISH
r	air⁻ay

ENGLISH	SPANISH
rr	airr⁻ay

<table>
<tr><td>ENGLISH</td><td>SPANISH</td></tr>
<tr><td>s</td><td>ay¯say</td></tr>
</table>

Trace the word.

ay¯say   ay¯say   ay¯say

Rewrite the word.

<table>
<tr><td>ENGLISH</td><td>SPANISH</td></tr>
<tr><td>t</td><td>tay</td></tr>
</table>

Trace the word.

tay   tay   tay

Rewrite the word.

<table>
<tr><th>ENGLISH</th><th>SPANISH</th></tr>
<tr><td>u</td><td>oo</td></tr>
</table>

Trace the word.

Rewrite the word.

<table>
<tr><th>ENGLISH</th><th>SPANISH</th></tr>
<tr><td>v</td><td>bay chee-kah</td></tr>
</table>

Trace the word.

baychee-kah   baychee-kah

Rewrite the word.

<table><tr><td>ENGLISH</td><td>SPANISH</td></tr></table>

ENGLISH	SPANISH
w	bay doh-blay

 Trace the word.

bay doh-blay   bay doh-blay

 Rewrite the word.

ENGLISH	SPANISH
x	ah-kees

 Trace the word.

ah-kees   ah-kees   ah-kees

 Rewrite the word.

<table>
<tr><td>ENGLISH</td><td>SPANISH</td></tr>
<tr><td>y</td><td>ee-gree-ay-gah</td></tr>
</table>

Trace the word.

ee gree ay gah   ee gree ay gah

Rewrite the word.

<table>
<tr><td>ENGLISH</td><td>SPANISH</td></tr>
<tr><td>z</td><td>say-tah</td></tr>
</table>

Trace the word.

say tah   say tah   say tah

Rewrite the word.

Let's learn the Spanish numbers.

ARABIC	SPANISH
0	**cero**
	say-roh

✏️ Trace the word.

cero   cero   cero

✏️ Rewrite the word.

ARABIC	SPANISH
1	**uno**
	oo-noh

✏️ Trace the word.

uno   uno   uno

✏️ Rewrite the word.

<table>
<tr><td>ARABIC</td><td>SPANISH</td></tr>
</table>

2

dos

dohs

Trace the word.

d o s   d o s   d o s

Rewrite the word.

<table>
<tr><td>ARABIC</td><td>SPANISH</td></tr>
</table>

3

tres

trays

Trace the word.

tres   tres   tres

Rewrite the word.

ARABIC	SPANISH
4	**cuatro**
	kwah-troh

✏️ Trace the word.

cuatro   cuatro   cuatro

✏️ Rewrite the word.

ARABIC	SPANISH
5	**cinco**
	seen-koh

✏️ Trace the word.

cinco   cinco   cinco

✏️ Rewrite the word.

ARABIC	SPANISH
6	**seis**
	says

Trace the word.

seis   seis   seis

Rewrite the word.

ARABIC	SPANISH
7	**siete**
	see-ay-tay

Trace the word.

siete   siete   siete

Rewrite the word.

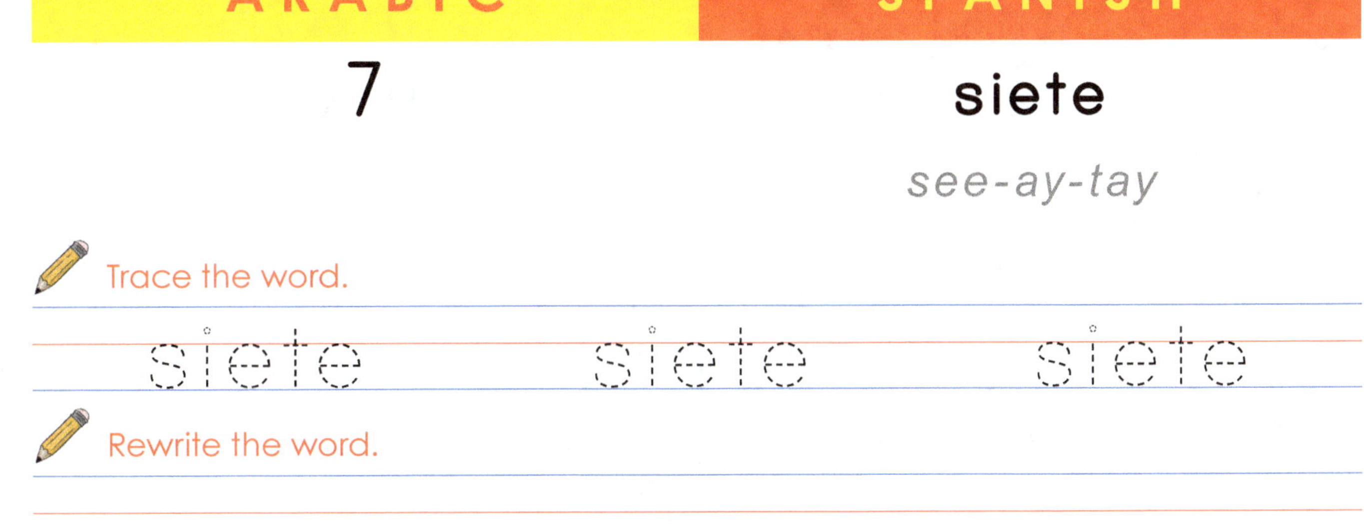

ARABIC	SPANISH
8	**ocho**

oh-choh

✏️ Trace the word.

ocho   ocho   ocho

✏️ Rewrite the word.

ARABIC	SPANISH
9	**nueve**

new-ay-vay

✏️ Trace the word.

nueve   nueve   nueve

✏️ Rewrite the word.

ARABIC	SPANISH
10	**diez**
	dee-ays

✏️ Trace the word.

diez   diez   diez

✏️ Rewrite the word.

ARABIC	SPANISH
11	**once**
	ohn-say

✏️ Trace the word.

once   once   once

✏️ Rewrite the word.

ARABIC	SPANISH

12

doce

doh-say

✏️ Trace the word.

doce   doce   doce

✏️ Rewrite the word.

ARABIC	SPANISH

13

trece

tray-say

✏️ Trace the word.

trece   trece   trece

✏️ Rewrite the word.

<table>
<tr><td>ARABIC</td><td>SPANISH</td></tr>
</table>

14

catorce

kah-tor-say

 Trace the word.

catorce   catorce   catorce

 Rewrite the word.

<table>
<tr><td>ARABIC</td><td>SPANISH</td></tr>
</table>

15

quince

keen-say

 Trace the word.

 quince   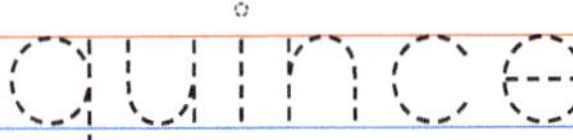 quince   quince

 Rewrite the word.

<table>
<tr><td>ARABIC</td><td>SPANISH</td></tr>
</table>

ARABIC | SPANISH

16

diez y seis

dee-ays ee says

Trace the word.

diez y seis   diez y seis

Rewrite the word.

ARABIC | SPANISH

17

diez y siete

dee-ays ee see-ay-tay

Trace the word.

diez y siete   diez y siete

Rewrite the word.

18

diez y ocho

dee-ays ee oh-choh

✏️ Trace the word.

diez y ocho   diez y ocho

✏️ Rewrite the word.

19

diez y nueve

dee-ays ee new-ay-vay

✏️ Trace the word.

diez y nueve   diez y nueve

✏️ Rewrite the word.

ARABIC	SPANISH
20	**veinte**
	bayn-tay

✏️ Trace the word.

veinte   veinte   veinte

✏️ Rewrite the word.

ARABIC	SPANISH
100	**cien(to)**
	see-ain-(toh)

✏️ Trace the word.

cien(to)   cien(to)   cien(to)

✏️ Rewrite the word.

Let's learn some basic Spanish phrases.

<table>
<tr><td>ENGLISH</td><td>SPANISH</td></tr>
</table>

Good morning!

¡Buenos días!

bway-nohs dee-ahs

 Trace the word.

¡Buenos días!

 Rewrite the word.

<table>
<tr><td>ENGLISH</td><td>SPANISH</td></tr>
</table>

Thank you (very much).

(Muchas) Gracias.

(moo-chahs) grah-see-ahs

 Trace the word.

(Muchas) Gracias.

 Rewrite the word.

ENGLISH	SPANISH
I'm sorry	Lo siento

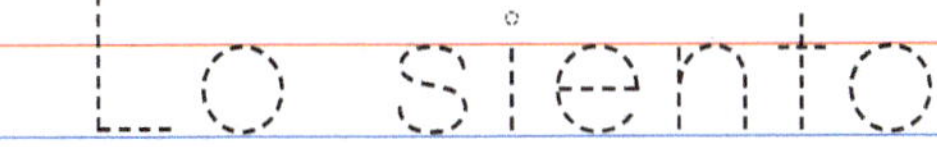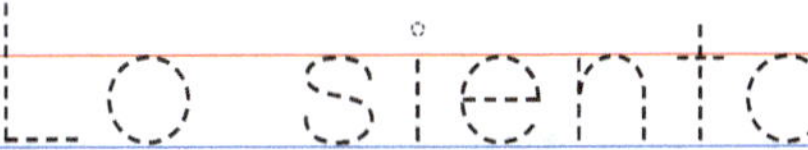

loh see-ehn-toh

 Trace the word.

Lo siento   Lo siento

Rewrite the word.

ENGLISH	SPANISH
How are you?	¿Cómo está usted?

koh-moh ay-stah oo-sted

Trace the word.

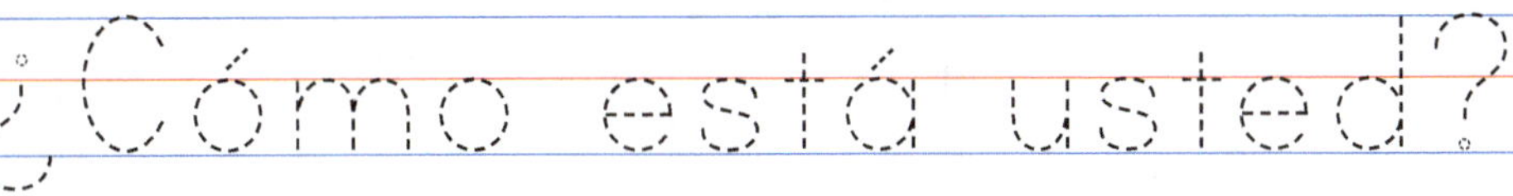

¿Cómo está usted?

 Rewrite the word.

<table>
<tr><td>

</td><td>

</td></tr>
</table>

ENGLISH	SPANISH
What is your name?	¿Cómo se llama usted?
	koh-moh say yah-mah oo-sted

 Trace the word.

¿Cómo se llama usted?

 Rewrite the word.

ENGLISH	SPANISH
Nice to meet you.	Mucho gusto.
	moo-choh goo-stoh

 Trace the word.

Mucho gusto. Mucho gusto.

 Rewrite the word.

<table>
<tr><td>ENGLISH</td><td>SPANISH</td></tr>
</table>

Good afternoon!

¡Buenas tardes!

bway-nahs tard-ays

 Trace the word.

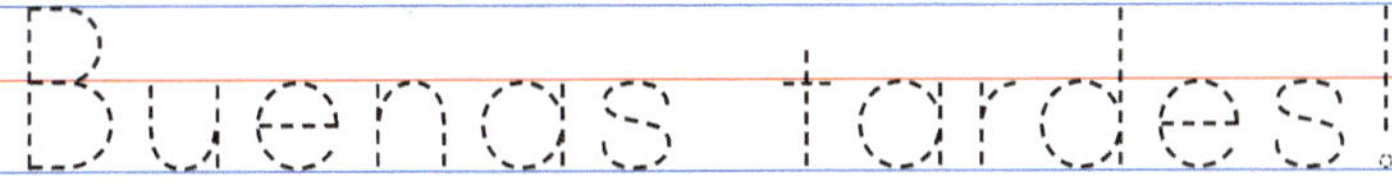

 Rewrite the word.

<table>
<tr><td>ENGLISH</td><td>SPANISH</td></tr>
</table>

Good bye.

Adiós.

ah-dee-ohs

 Trace the word.

 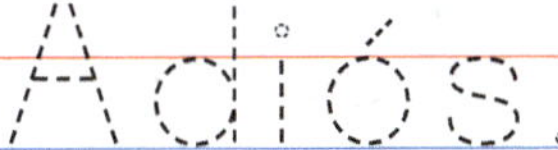 

 Rewrite the word.

<table>
<tr><td></td><td></td></tr>
</table>

ENGLISH

You're welcome.

SPANISH

De nada.

day nah-dah

 Trace the word.

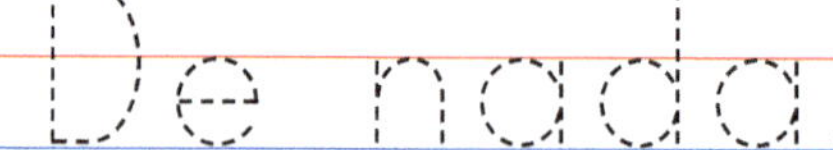

 Rewrite the word.

ENGLISH

Good evening!

SPANISH

¡Buenas noches!

bway-nahs noh-chays

 Trace the word.

 Rewrite the word.

<table>
<tr><td></td><td></td></tr>
</table>

ENGLISH	SPANISH
Please.	Por favor.
	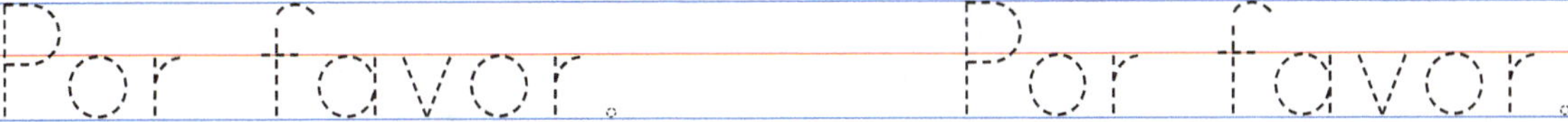 *por fah-bor*

 Trace the word.

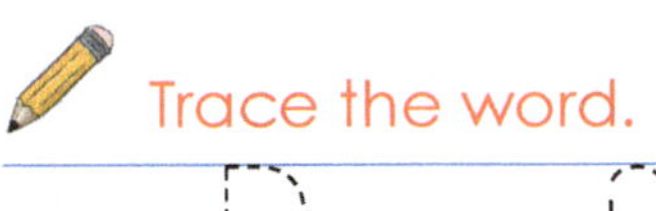 Por favor.   Por favor.

Rewrite the word.

ENGLISH	SPANISH
See you tomorrow.	Hasta mañana.
	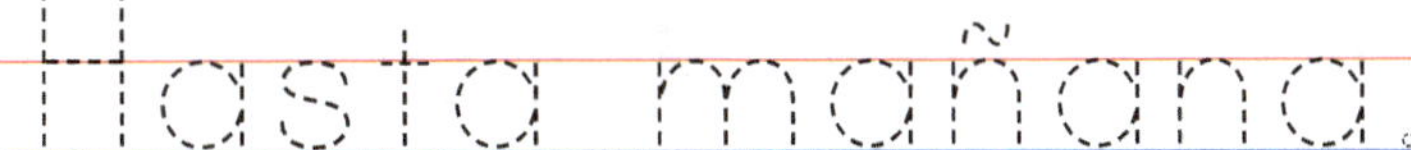 *ah-stah mahn-yahn-ah*

 Trace the word.

 Hasta mañana.

Rewrite the word.

<table>
<tr><td>ENGLISH</td><td>SPANISH</td></tr>
<tr><td>How are you?</td><td>¿Cómo estás?
koh-moh ay-stahs</td></tr>
</table>

 Trace the word.

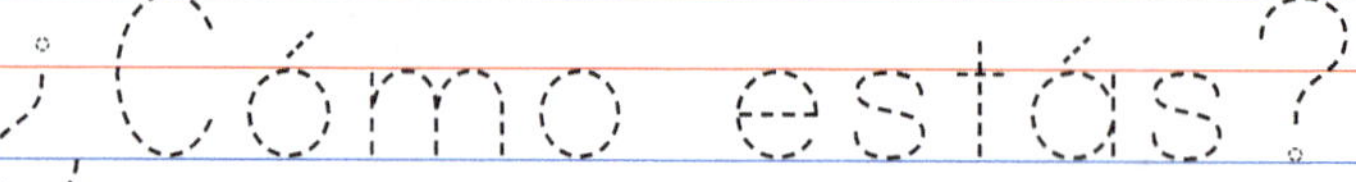

 Rewrite the word.

<table>
<tr><td>ENGLISH</td><td>SPANISH</td></tr>
<tr><td>Let's go!</td><td>¡Vamos!
bah-mohs</td></tr>
</table>

 Trace the word.

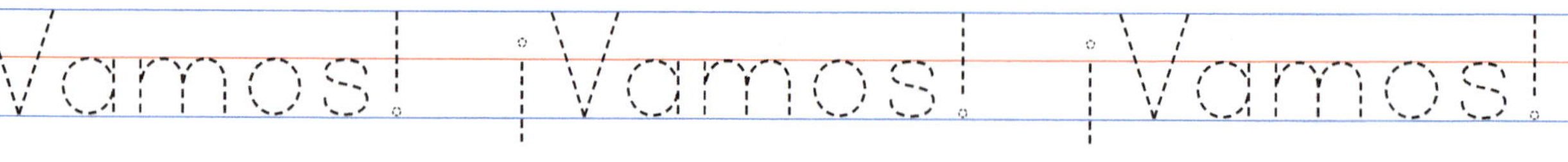

Rewrite the word.

<table>
<tr><th>ENGLISH</th><th>SPANISH</th></tr>
<tr><td>Have a nice day!</td><td>¡Que le vaya bien!
keh leh vah-yah bee-ehn</td></tr>
</table>

Trace the word.

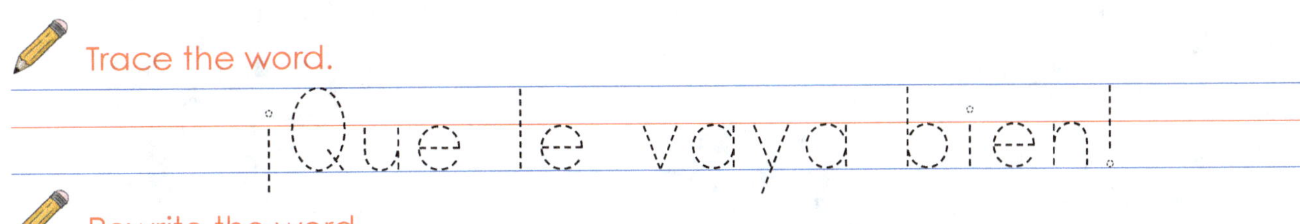

Rewrite the word.

<table>
<tr><th>ENGLISH</th><th>SPANISH</th></tr>
<tr><td>I love you.</td><td>Te amo.
tay ah-moh</td></tr>
</table>

Trace the word.

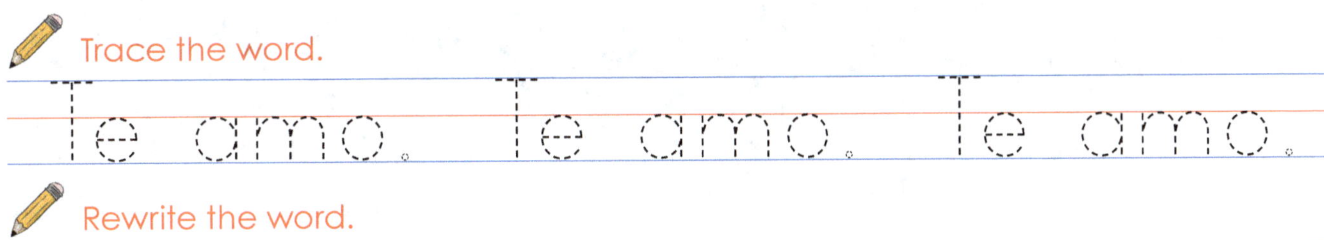

Rewrite the word.

Visit
BABY PROFESSOR
EDUCATION KIDS
www.BabyProfessorBooks.com
to download Free Baby Professor eBooks
and view our catalog of new and exciting
Children's Books